Truck Drive

A Bumper Collection

By Cheste.

Jokes For Truck Drivers

These jokes for truck drivers will make you giggle. Some of these jokes are old, some of them are new and we hope you enjoy our collection of the very best truck driver jokes and puns around.

You will find some great truck driver jokes all guaranteed to get you laughing out loud. Hopefully they won't drive you around the bend.

Published by Glowworm Press
7 Nuffield Way
Abingdon OX14 1RL

FOREWORD

When I was asked to write a foreword to this book I was chuffed.

That is until I was told that I was the last resort by the author, Chester Croker, and that everyone else he had approached had said they couldn't do it!

I will give him a *brake* though, as he *wipes me out* with his gags, and I often end up *exhausted* with laughter.

I have known Chester for a number of years and his ability to create funny jokes is absolutely incredible. He is quick witted and an expert at crafting amusing puns.

He will be glad you have bought this book, as he has an expensive lifestyle to maintain.

Enjoy!

Captain Cargo

Table of Contents

Chapter 1: Truck Driver Jokes

If you're looking for truck driver jokes and funny truck driver related jokes you've certainly come to the right place.

In this book you will find corny truck driver jokes that will make you laugh. Some of these truckers jokes are old, some of them are new, and this mixture of jokes will prove truck drivers have a good sense of humor, and they are guaranteed to get you laughing.

We've got some great one-liners to start with, plenty of quick fire question and answer themed gags, some story led jokes and as a bonus some cheesy pick-up lines for truckers.

Chapter 2: One Liner Trucker Jokes

A painter and decorator had his vehicle stolen and all he could say was "Where did my Van Gogh?"

A Wilkinson Sword lorry almost crashed into a Gillette truck earlier today. Both drivers said it was the closest shave they've ever had.

Truckers have been getting in trouble with the environmentalists for animal cruelty, but their trucks don't even go fast enough to kill the bugs – just fast enough to break their little arms and legs.

My wife had her truck driving test last week.

She got eight out of ten.

The other two guys jumped clear.

Best truck I have seen is from a digestive company. It takes the biscuit.

My wife gave birth in a state-of-the-art delivery room," one trucker told another. "It was so high tech that our baby girl came out cordless."

Two cheese trucks ran into each other. De brie was everywhere.

Every trucker out there has an opinion on whether gasoline or diesel trucks are better. No matter the truck, you still need some motion lotion to keep you going!

A truck carrying yo-yos drove off a cliff into the sea and drowned.

73 times so far.

Sometimes trucks with just one trailer wiggle, so it makes sense the more trailers there are, the more wiggling that will happen.

If you don't know where you are going, any road will get you there.

I don't think there's any real motivation for somebody to be a truck driver. Mine was simple; my Dad was a truck driver, I wanted to own one.

You would never see me driving around in a sports car. I feel like you're so low and squishable by transport trucks.

A truck load of mixed peppercorns has crashed on the highway; traffic in the area has ground to a halt.

The wooziest thing a guy can do is drive a clean truck. Dents, scratches and mud - that's manly.

I just blew a tranny and an engine in my truck both in the same week. Boy, it really ruined my day when they found out about each other.

Did you hear about the work-shy trucker who ran out of sick days, so he called in dead.

A truck driver's wife asked him to pass her lipstick last week but he passed her a glue stick instead by mistake. She still isn't talking to him.

A truck load of glue has spilled onto the highway; traffic in the area is stuck.

It takes 8,460 bolts to assemble a truck, but only one nut to scatter it all over the road.

A truck carrying strawberries crashed earlier today. It created a huge jam.

He who hesitates is not only lost but several miles from the next freeway exit.

Yo mama so fat, that when she gets in a monster truck, it becomes a low-rider.

There is more credit and satisfaction in being a first-rate truck driver than a tenth-rate executive.

A truck has spilled a load of liquid chocolate. The road is a sticky mess, and traffic in the area is choc-a-block.

Did you hear about the truck driver who stole a calendar? He got twelve months.

A friend of mine once had sex with an exhaust pipe on a truck. He later found out he was HGV positive.

A truck carrying 100 pallets of Viagra was stolen last night. The Police are searching for a gang of hardened criminals.

I got called pretty yesterday and it felt good. Actually, the full sentence was "You're a pretty bad truck driver." but I'm focusing on the positive.

With the rise of self-driving vehicles, it's only a matter of time before we get a country song where a guy's truck leaves him.

A truck load of tortoises crashed into another truck carrying terrapins. It was a turtle disaster.

A truck crashed earlier today, covering the road in Vick's vapor rub. Don't worry though - there was no congestion at all.

Did you hear about the cross-eyed truck driver who got sacked because he couldn't see eye to eye with his boss.

I drove past a truck carrying canned orange juice and I almost got into an accident. I should have concentrated on the road.

A truck load of wigs was stolen last night.

Police are combing the area.

A lorry full of snooker equipment toppled over onto the road. There were cues in all directions.

I saw a programme on the TV about a truck load of shoemakers. What a load of cobblers.

I saw a truck carrying pens have a serious crash. It was a write off.

Amazon Prime say that they offer same-day delivery, so why did my parcel arrive at night?

The journey of a thousand miles begins with a broken fan belt and a leaky tire.

As a truck driver I know the value of putting something away for a rainy day.

I've gone for an umbrella.

Chapter 3: Q&A Truck Driver Jokes

Q: What do you call a JB Hunt Truck with a reefer unit?

A: *Prime*

Q: Why do some Roadway Trucks have only one seat?

A: *So the driver knows which side to get in.*

Q: Do you know what those long skid marks are that you see along highways?

A: *A Schneider driver that's run out of hours.*

Q: How do you make a million dollars from trucking?

A: *Start with two million.*

Q: Why don't we see many women in the trucking business?

A: *Because they take nine months to deliver their load.*

Q: What's the difference between a Jehovah's Witness and a Freightliner?

A: *At least you can close the door on the Jehovah's Witness.*

Q: Why does JB Hunt paint their truck frames orange?

A: *So when they roll their truck everyone will think it's a Schneider truck.*

Q: Schneider is planning to buy the trucking company "Overnight."

A: *They plan to change the name of the company to "Sometime next week."*

Q: What do you get when Swift leaves a truck stop?

A: *Two parking spaces.*

Q: Why Are Truckers Like Dogs?

A: *They wee on tires, chase cars, live in a box, and once in a while get to bury the bone.*

Q: What does Roadway really stand for?

A: *Really old *** driver working another year.*

Q: What does Werner really stand for?

A: *We employ rednecks; no experience required.*

Q: What does CRST really stand for?

A: *Caution really slow truck.*

Q: How do truckers contact each other in Wisconsin?

A: *They use a Milwaukee-Talkie.*

Q: What has one horn and provides milk?

A: *A dairy truck.*

Q: What kind of vehicle does Iron Man drive?

A: *Iron Van.*

Q: How Do You Say JB Hunt In German?

A: *Schneider.*

Q: What's the difference between a Peterbilt and a Porcupine?

A: *On the porcupine the Peter is on the outside.*

Q: What does a Schneider truck and an orange barrel have in common?

A: *They both have a dirt bag in them.*

Q: What kind of truck does Santa drive?

A: *A sleighteen wheeler.*

Q: Did you hear that Navistar International and Mack are going to merge?

A: *The new truck will be called a Corn-Dog.*

Q: What do you call a trucker who's happy every single Monday morning?

A: *Retired.*

Q: Why do truck drivers like wearing finger-less gloves?

A: *They like to see their girlfriends in shorts*

Q: What happens when five Aldi drivers leave a truck stop?

A: *You get ten extra parking spaces.*

Q: Why do truck drivers love the 1st August so much?

A: *It's only four more sleeps til Christmas.*

Q: What do you call an old trucker that doesn't drive trucks much anymore?

A: *Semi- retired.*

Chapter 4: Short Truck Driver Jokes

An elderly couple goes to Burger King and shares their fries and burger. A trucker sitting next to them offers to pay for the old lady.

"It's all right," says the elderly man. "We always share everything."

On seeing that the old lady has not eaten anything, the trucker once again makes an offer.

The old man once again assures the trucker to stay calm and resumes eating.

Finally, the trucker asks the lady why she is not eating anything.

The old lady replies, "I am waiting for the teeth."

A truck driver is off duty and is struggling to find a parking space at the mall.

"Lord," he prayed. "I can't stand this. If you open a space up for me, I swear I'll give up the booze and go to church every Sunday."

Suddenly, the clouds part and the sun shines down onto an empty parking spot. Without hesitation, the trucker says: "Never mind Lord, I found one."

The trucker complained to his buddy that his wife didn't satisfy him anymore.

His friend advised he find another woman on the side, on the double.

When they met up a month or so later, the trucker told his friend, "I took your advice. I managed to find a woman on the side, but my wife still doesn't satisfy me!"

A young truck driver is sitting at the bar one night, when a big scary, hairy construction worker sits down next to him.

They have a few drinks and after a while the conversation moves on to nuclear war.

The truck driver asks the construction worker, "If you hear the sirens go off, the missiles are on their way, and you've only got 20 minutes left to live, what would you do?"

The construction worker replies, "That's easy - I'm gonna make it with anything that moves."

The construction worker then asks the truck driver what he would do to which he replies, "I'm gonna try and keep perfectly still."

A trucker was applying for a job in a huge MNC. In the interview, the interviewer asked him, "Suppose you both are carrying a highly flammable liquid through the night. Out of the blue at 2am, a speeding car comes and hits your trailer. What would be the first thing you do?"

The trucker replies "Well, I'd wake my partner Joey first. He would love to see this movie like explosion first hand."

A truck driver didn't notice a 'low bridge ahead' sign and got stuck under the bridge.

A police officer arrives and says to the truck driver, "Have you got stuck?"

The truck driver replies, "No, I was delivering this bridge and ran out of gas."

As I was driving to work this morning, this truck driver swerved right through the traffic, cutting up the other road users before smashing into the back of a car.

On the back of his truck was a sign saying, 'How am I driving?' and I thought to myself, "I've got no idea either."

A married woman gets hit by a truck and the cops tell her husband, "Sir, it looks like your wife's been hit by a truck."

The husband replies, "I know, but she has a great personality and she's good with the kids."

A truck driver tries to enter a smart bar wearing a shirt open at the collar, and is met by a bouncer who tells him that he must wear a necktie to gain admission.

So the truck driver goes back to his vehicle and gets some jump leads, and manages to fashion a knot and lets the ends dangle free.

He goes back to the bar and the bouncer carefully looks him over, and then says, "Well, OK, I guess you can come in now – but just don't start anything!"

A dog walks into a bar and says to the barman, "Can I have a pint of lager and a packet of nuts please."

The barman has never seen or heard a talking dog before and says, "Wow, that's amazing - you should join the circus."

The talking dog replies, "Why? Do they need truck drivers?"

A trucker took his cross-eyed dog to the vet.

The vet picked the dog up to examine him and said, "Sorry, I'm going to have to put him down."

The trucker said "Oh, it's not that bad is it?"

The vet replied, "No, he's just very heavy."

A proud father is showing pictures of his three sons to an old friend and he is asked, "What do your boys do for a living?

He replied, "Well my youngest is a neurosurgeon and my middle is a lawyer."

"What does the oldest child do?" his friend asked.

The reply came, "He's the truck driver that paid for the others' education."

A friend of mine was run over by a red lorry, then a yellow lorry, then a red lorry, then a yellow lorry.

When the policeman informed his family he said, "There's no easy way to say this."

A lorry driver gets lost one day and as luck would have it he finds a low bridge and gets stuck under it. The cars are backed up for miles behind him.

Eventually, a police car pulls up. The police officer gets out and walks around to the lorry driver.

The cop puts his hands on his hips and says to the driver, "Got stuck huh, sir?"

The lorry driver replies, "No, I was delivering this bridge and ran out of gas."

This trucker goes into a brothel one day and puts $300 on the counter. Then he says to the madam, "I want the ugliest girl in the place and a ham sandwich."

The madam of the house looks at the big wad of money in front of her and says to him, "You know, for $300 you could have the most beautiful girl in here."

The trucker looks at her and replies, "Listen, I'm not horny, I'm home sick."

A trucker meets up with his latest dumb blonde girlfriend as she is picking up her car from the auto repair shop.

He asks her, "Everything ok with your car now?"

"Yes, thank goodness," the dipsy blonde replies.

He asks her, "Weren't you a little worried that the mechanic might rip you off?"

The blonde says, "Yes, but he didn't. I was so pleased when he told me that all I needed was some blinker fluid!"

A truck driver was pulled over by a State Trooper.

The patrolman told him to get out of the truck, and he noticed that as the driver stepped out of the cab, he appeared to put something in his mouth.

Thinking that the driver was taking some pep pills, the patrolman said, "Did I just see you swallow something?"

The truck driver replied, "Yeah, that was my birth control pill."

"Your birth control pill?" asked the patrolman.

The trucker said, "Yeah, when I saw your flashing light, I knew I was screwed."

Walking into a lawyer's office, a truck driver asks, "How much do you charge?"

"Two hundred and fifty dollars for three questions." the lawyer stated.

"Isn't that rather expensive?" the truck driver asked.

"Yes," the lawyer replied. "What's your third question?"

An old trucker went to his doctor with a hearing problem.

The doctor says, "Can you describe the symptoms to me?"

The trucker replies, "Yes I can. Homer is a fat yellow lazy man and his wife Marge is skinny with big blue hair."

A retired truck driver was walking along the road one day when he came across a frog.

He reached down, picked up the frog, and began to put it in his pocket. As he did so, the frog said to him, "Kiss me on the lips and I'll turn into a beautiful woman and show you a good time."

The old trucker carried on putting the frog in his pocket.

The frog said, "Didn't you hear what I just said?"

The trucker looked at the frog and said, "Yes, but at my age I'd rather have a talking frog."

A trucker had driven straight for 16 hours.

He was tired and so he stopped to get some sleep. As he was sleeping, his slumber was disturbed by a knock on the window.

He got up to find a young jogger asking him what time it was. He told him that it was 5:15 am and went back to sleep.

Minutes later another jogger approached and asked the time. Irritated, the trucker told him the time and decided to put up a sign saying he didn't know the time on his window and went back to sleep.

About an hour later, there was a knock on the window and a jogger said, "It's 6:25 am brother."

A young trucker safety group goes on a reality field trip to the police station.

The Desk Officer points to the ten most wanted list and tells them that these are the most wanted bad guys in the country.

One junior trucker asks, "These are the most wanted men in the country huh?"

The desk officer said, "Yes."

One of the junior truckers then asks, "Why didn't you keep them locked up when you took their mug shots?!"

I was walking down the street earlier today when a truck driver pulled up alongside me and said, "Excuse me; I'm looking for the accident site involving a truck carrying a load of cutlery."

"No problem," I said. "Go straight down this road for a mile, then take the first left, and when you get to the fork in the road you're there."

A truck driver called Paddy calls up his local paper and asks, "How much would it be to put an ad in your paper?"

"Four dollars an inch," a woman replies. "Why? What are you selling?"

"A four-foot high cab ladder," said Paddy before slamming the phone down.

While driving along the back roads of a small town, two truckers came to an overpass with a sign that read CLEARANCE 11'3".

They got out and measured their rig, which was 12'4".

"What do you think?" one asked the other.

The driver looked around carefully, then shifted into first. "Not a cop in sight. Let's take a chance!"

Chapter 5: Longer Truck Driver Jokes

Three Friends

Ron is talking to two of his pals, Jim and Shamus.

Jim says, "I think my wife is having an affair with a truck driver. The other day I came home and found a tire thumper under our bed and it wasn't mine."

Shamus then confides, "Well, I think my wife is having an affair with an electrician. The other day I found some wire cutters under the bed and they weren't mine."

Ron then says, "You know – I think my wife is having an affair with a horse."

Both Jim and Shamus look at him in disbelief.

Ron sees them looking at him and says, "No, seriously. The other day I came home early and found a jockey under our bed."

Pulling Power

Carlo the property developer and his truck driver buddy Sam, went bar-hopping every week together, and every week Carlo would go home with a woman while Sam went home alone.

One week Sam asked Carlo his secret to picking up women. "That's easy," said Carlo "When she asks you what you do for a living, don't tell her you're a trucker. Tell her you're a lawyer."

Later Sam is dancing with a woman when she leans in and asks him what he does for a living.

"I'm a lawyer," says Sam.

The woman smiles and asks, "Want to go back to my place? It's just around the corner."

So, they go to her place, have some fun and an hour later, Sam is back in the pub telling Carlo about his success.

"I've only been a lawyer for an hour," Sam snickered, "And I've already screwed someone!"

Hairy Bikers

A trucker stopped at a roadside diner one day to grab some lunch. He ordered a cheeseburger, a coffee and a slice of apple pie.

Just as he was about to eat them, three big hairy bikers walked in.

The first biker grabbed the trucker's cheeseburger and took a big bite from it.

The second biker picked up the trucker's coffee and downed it in one gulp.

The third biker ate the trucker's apple pie.

The truck driver didn't do anything or say a word as all this went on.

When they finished, he just paid the waitress and left.

The first biker said to the waitress, "He is not much of a man, is he?"

"He's not much of a driver, either," the waitress replied. "He's just backed his 18-wheeler over three motorbikes."

The Moustache

A trucker's wife was having an affair with a guy with a big moustache. The two lovebirds were getting it together when the trucker came back from his delivery trip early without informing the wife.

When he knocked on the door, the wife saw him through the peep hole and hid her lover under the bed. She greeted her husband at the door and asked him why her honey had come back so early.

He said, "Well, my boss, the ugly one with the fat moustache wouldn't let me go, so I came here to get my gun and kill him!"

Unexpectedly, the lover from under the bed came running out and ran off from the door.

The trucker, with astonishment on his face, said, "I was not talking about that moustached fellow, but my boss is going to be the second moustached guy I am going to shoot today."

The Farmer's Fields

It was a bright sunny summer's day, and a farmer was busy tending his fields when a trucker rolled up and said, "Hey farmer, that's some mighty fine honeysuckle you've got there. Mind if I grab myself some jars of honey?"

The farmer, thinking the trucker a fool, said "Sure, you go right ahead."

An hour later the trucker came back with jars filled to the brim with honey.

The trucker left, leaving the farmer shocked.

The next day, the trucker rolled up again and said, "Hey farmer, that's some mighty fine milkweed you've got there. Mind if I help myself to some milk?"

Believing that the trucker couldn't pull off the same feat twice, the farmer once again let him go ahead into his field.

An hour later the trucker came back, jugs of milk splashing about in his arms.

The trucker drove away and the farmer was, again, left shocked.

The next day, the trucker rolled up again and said, "Hey farmer, that's some mighty fine pussywillow you've got there. Mind if I help myself to some?"

The farmer quickly replied, "Hold on - I'm coming with you this time!"

Losing A Load

It was snowing heavily and a trucker was driving along. While he was stopped at a red light a blonde ran up to him and knocked on his window. When he lowered his window, she said, "Hi my name is Sally and you are losing your load from the back of the truck."

The trucker nods and goes back to his work. He continued to drive on, but at the next red light, the same blonde runs up to him, and knocks on his window and when he lowered it, she said, "Hi my name is Sally, and you are losing your load from the back of the truck", in a tone like nothing had happened at the last signal.

This continued for the next two signals when finally the trucker decided he has had enough.

So at the next red light, as soon as he stopped, he ran to the blonde's car and knocked on her window and said, "Hi my name is Tommy and I am driving a salt truck to sprinkle on the ice."

The Priest

Henry was a trucker and he was good at his job, but he had developed an intense hate for lawyers. While driving his truck, he would go out of his way to hit a lawyer to satisfy himself.

One day when he was on his way to deliver a cargo, he saw a priest walking down the road and decided to give him a lift and drop him off at his destination.

Later, as the priest was sitting on the shotgun seat and the truck was driving along, the driver saw a lawyer walking by the road.

His instinct kicked him and he swerved to hit him but realizing that he was with a priest, he immediately swerved back, narrowly missing the lawyer.

However, he heard a loud thud. He was looking back in the mirror when he said, "Phew, I almost hit that lawyer."

The priest turned towards him and said, "Lucky us. I managed to hit him with my door."

Raincoat Guys

A guy is driving his truck through a storm when he notices a man wearing a red raincoat on the side of the road waving at him, so he pulls over.

He lowers the window and asks, 'What do you want?'

He gets the reply, 'I'm the red-coated dickhead, and I'm very hungry!'

The trucker hands out a sandwich to the guy and then drives on.

Soon, he sees a man in a yellow raincoat on the side of the road waving at him, so he pulls over once more.

He lowers the window and asks, 'What do you want?'

He gets the reply, 'I'm the yellow-coated dickhead, and I'm very thirsty!'

The trucker hands out a bottle of water to the guy and drives on.

Soon, he sees another guy on the side of the road waving at him, this time wearing a black raincoat, so he pulls over again.

He lowers the window and asks, 'And you, you black-coated dickhead, what the f*ck do you want?

He gets the reply, 'License and registration.'

Shotgun Girl

John, an experienced truck driver, was on his way to pick up his next shipment when he saw a young, pretty lady asking for a ride on the side of the highway.

Sure enough, John was kind enough to give her a ride. When the girl was climbing in the shotgun seat, the trucker introduced himself as 'John Snow.' and she introduced herself as 'June Watson.'

As they were driving along, John would occasionally take a peek at the pretty girl, who was wearing a mini skirt and a crop top.

After she realized what John was doing, she asked, "Why do you glance at me all the time, John?"

John chuckled and said, "Can you imagine having seven inches of Snow in June? That's why."

The Happy Camper

Tony was on his camping trip when he got lost and separated from his group. He ate from the wild and got an upset stomach and needed to poop really often. He came across a diner where he asked for a lift. A trucker agreed to help him and said he'd drop him off at the nearest town, but that he wouldn't stop anywhere in-between. Not having many options, Tony hopped in the truck.

An hour into the ride, he felt like pooping. He asked the driver to stop, but the driver said, "If you have to go so bad, stick your ass out the window and poo."

Tony did as he was told and as the truck was speeding along, his sh*t sprayed onto two people walking along the road.

The first walker wiped his face and said, "Goddammit, what are truck drivers chewing these days?"

His friend responded, "Forget that, did you see the lips of that trucker?"

Bird Flu

Researchers found over 200 dead crows on the highway last year, and there was concern that they may have died from Avian Flu.

A bird pathologist examined the remains of all the crows, and, to everyone's relief, confirmed the problem was definitely NOT Avian Flu and he assigned the cause of death to be vehicular impacts.

However, during the detailed analysis it was noted that varying colors of paints appeared on the bird's beaks and claws. By analyzing these paint residues it was determined that 95% of the crows had been killed by impact with trucks, while only 5% were killed by an impact with a car.

An ornithological behaviorist was called to determine if there was a cause for the disproportionate percentages of truck kills versus car kills.

The bird behaviorist quickly concluded the cause: when crows eat road kill, they always have a look-out crow in a nearby tree to warn of impending danger.

The scientific conclusion was that while all the lookout crows could call out "Cah", none could call out "Truck."

The Old Man

A guy is in a bar when he sees an old man crying his yes out, so he asks the old man what's the matter.

"I've had a great life," says the old man. "I ran a successful haulage company which I sold for a lot of money."

The guy says, "So what's the problem?"

The old man snuffles into his sleeve and says, "I built myself a huge mansion with a swimming pool."

The guy says, "Okay, so what's the problem?"

The old man wails and says, "I own a beautiful car."

The guy looks puzzled and says, "I don't see what the problem is."

The old man blows his nose and says, "Last month I got married to a 25 year old Playboy bunny."

The guy loses his temper. "So, what is the problem?"

The old man sobs, "I can't remember where I live!

The Penguins

A trucker had bid to get the shipment of 800 penguins to the zoo. After winning the bid, as he was loading the animals into the truck, he realized that only 600 penguins would fit into his truck.

So he called a fellow trucker and said, "Hey man, Can you take 200 penguins to the zoo for me?"

The other trucker agreed and loaded the 200 penguins into his truck.

The next day, when the first trucker arrived at the zoo, he saw a long line of penguins led by his fellow truck driver going out of the zoo.

He confronted his fellow trucker and asked him what he was doing. He replied, "Well I took them to the zoo as you asked and now I have some cash left over so we are going to see a movie."

Truckers Reunion Lunch

A group of truckers, all aged 40, discussed where they should meet for a reunion lunch. They agreed they would meet at a place called Sally's Diner because the place had a great atmosphere, and the barmaids had big breasts and wore short-skirts.

Ten years later, all aged 50, the truckers once again discussed where they should meet for lunch.

It was agreed that they would meet at Sally's Diner because the food and service was good and there was an excellent beer selection.

Ten years later, at age 60, the friends discussed where they should meet for lunch.

It was agreed that they would meet at Sally's Diner because there were plenty of parking spaces, they could dine in peace and quiet, and it was good value for money.

Ten years later, at age 70, the friends discussed where they should meet for lunch.

It was agreed that they would meet at Sally's Diner because the restaurant was wheelchair accessible and had a toilet for the disabled.

Ten years later, at age 80, the old truckers discussed where they should meet for lunch.

Finally it was agreed that they would meet at Sally's Diner because they had never been there before.

Three Daughters

A trucker was talking to two of his friends about their teenage daughters.

The first friend says "I was cleaning my daughter's room the other day and I found a pack of cigarettes. I didn't even know she smoked."

The second friend says, "That's nothing. I was cleaning my daughter's room the other day and I found a half full bottle of Vodka. I didn't even know she drank."

The trucker says, "That's nothing. I was cleaning my daughter's room the other day and I found a pack of condoms. I didn't even know she had a penis."

Three Flat Tires

A trucker came into a truck stop cafe and placed his order. He said, "I want three flat tires, a pair of headlights and a pair of running boards."

The brand new blonde waitress, not wanting to appear stupid, went to the kitchen and said to the cook, "This guy out there just ordered three flat tires, a pair of headlights and a pair of running boards. What does he think this place is - an auto parts store?"

"No," the cook said. "Three flat tires means three pancakes, a pair of headlights is two eggs sunny side up, and running boards are 2 slices of crisp bacon."

"Oh, OK." said the blonde. She thought about it for a moment and then spooned up a bowl of beans and gave it to the customer.

The trucker asked, "What are the beans for, blondie?"

She replied, "I thought while you were waiting for the flat tires, headlights and running boards, you might as well gas up!"

20 Tons of Canaries

A man was driving down the road behind an 18 wheeler, and at every stoplight the trucker would get out of the cab, run back and bang on the trailer door.

After seeing this at several intersections in a row the motorist followed him until he pulled into a parking lot.

When they both had come to a stop, the truck driver once again jumped out and started banging on the trailer door.

The motorist went up to him and said, "I don't mean to be nosey but why do you keep banging on that door?" to which the trucker replied, "Sorry, can't talk now, I have 20 tons of canaries and a 10 ton limit, so I have to keep half of them flying at all times."

You Have The Brakes

A trucker who had driven his fully loaded rig to the top of a steep hill and was just starting down the equally steep other side when he noticed a man and a woman lying in the center of the road, making love.

He blew his air horn several times as he was bearing down on them.

Realizing that they were not about to get out of his way he slammed on his brakes and stopped just inches from them.

Getting out of the cab, the trucker stormed to the front of the cab and looked down at the two, still in the road, and yelled, "What the hell's the matter with you two? Didn't you hear me blowing the horn? You could've been killed!"

The man on the highway obviously satisfied, looked up and said, "Look, I was coming, she was coming, and you were coming. You were the only one with brakes."

Nerd Season

A trucker hauling computers and accessories is driving down the highway late one night when he sees a truck stop on the side of the road. So he decides to pull over. On approaching the door he reads a sign: "NO NERDS." He shrugs it off and enters. He's greeted by the end of a shotgun barrel in his face. "Are you a nerd?" the bartender asks.

"No, I`m a truck driver," he replies.

He's allowed to come in, so he orders a cup of coffee, sits at the bar and drinks it.

While he drinks his coffee, a man walks in wearing his pants up to his chest, a plaid shirt, pocket protector and thick-framed glass. The bartender pulls out his shotgun and blows him away.

"What the hell did you do that for?" asks the trucker.

"Well," the bartender answers, "it's nerd season."

"Nerd season?" asks the trucker, confused.

"Yeah. See, the nerd population in this town is getting out of hand, so we've opened up nerd season."

So, with that, he finishes his coffee and goes back on the road. While he is driving along, the car in front of him suddenly swerves and wrecks.

To avoid becoming part the disaster, the trucker swerves to get out of way, but the swerve is too hard and his tractor trailer flips and he dumps his load all over the road.

He gets out of his truck to see nerds coming from all directions grabbing everything they can.

Remembering what the bartender told him, he goes back to the truck and pulls out his gun and starts picking them off, one by one.

While he is shooting the nerds, a highway patrol officer starts running after him, waving his arms screaming, "Stop, stop!"

"What?" the trucker asks, confused, "I thought it was nerd season."

"Well yeah," the officer answers, "but you can't bait them!"

Trucker's Monkey

A trucker picks up a hitchhiker who climbs up in the cab and notices a monkey on the dashboard. After a few miles he asks the driver what the monkey is for.

The driver says, "I'll show you" and with that he hits the monkey with the back of his hand, sending the poor creature rolling across the dash.

The monkey goes down between the driver's legs, unzips his pants, pulls out his unit and proceeds to give the trucker head. When finished, the monkey pulls out a tissue, cleans the driver up, puts everything back and jumps back up on the dashboard.

"See that?" said the trucker.

The man replied "Yeah."

The trucker asked the hitchhiker, "You want to try it?"

The hitcher replied, "OK, but don't hit me as hard as you hit that monkey."

Train Passengers

A truck driver, a lawyer, a beautiful lady, and an old woman were on a train, sitting 2x2 facing each other.

The train went into a tunnel and when the carriage went totally dark, a "smack" was heard.

When the train came out of the tunnel back into the light the lawyer had a red hand print where he had been clearly slapped on his face.

The old lady thought, "That lawyer must have groped the young lady in the dark and she slapped him."

The hottie thought, "That lawyer must have tried to grope me, got the old lady by mistake, and she slapped him."

The lawyer thought, "That truck driver must have groped the hottie, she thought it was me, and slapped me."

The truck driver sat there thinking, "I can't wait for another tunnel so I can slap that lawyer again!"

Worker's Compensation

A truck driver who had been delivering radioactive waste for the local reactor begins to feel sick after a few years on the job and he decided to seek compensation for his ailment.

Upon his arrival at the workers' compensation department, he is interviewed by an assessor.

Assessor: "I see you work with radio-active materials and wish to claim compensation."

Trucker: "Yeah, I feel really sick."

Assessor: "Alright then, does your employer take measures to protect you from radiation poisoning?"

Trucker: "Yeah, he gives me a lead suit to wear on the job."

Assessor: "And what about the cabin in which you drive?"

Trucker: "Oh yeah. That's lead lined, all lead lined."

Assessor: "What about the waste itself? Where is that kept?"

Trucker: "Oh, the stuff is held in a lead container, all lead."

Assessor: "Let me see if I get this straight. You wear a lead suit, sit in a lead-lined cabin and the radio-active waste is kept in a lead container."

Trucker: "Yeah, that's right. All lead."

Assessor: "Then I can't see how you could claim against him for radiation poisoning."

Trucker: "I'm not. I'm claiming for lead poisoning."

Chapter 6: Truck Driver Pick-Up Lines

Would you like to lubricate my camshaft?

Is your battery dead? As I would love to jump you.

I need some coolant, because you've got my engine overheating.

I'm lost; can you tell me which road leads to your heart?

Do you mind if I check out your exhaust pipe?

I can't wait to unload.

Will I get a chance to pop your clutch?

Want to see my semi?

Those are some nice headlights, but there's no need to put your high beams on.

I have headlights too - wait until you see my high beam.

I built a sleeping bed in the back of my truck, seems there's too much room for one.

Want to get on my flat bed?

My batteries are designed for extended life.

Chapter 7: Bumper Stickers For Truck Drivers

I may be slow, but I'm ahead of you.

My driving scares me too.

Watch out - there's an idiot behind me.

Don't honk. Driver trying to sleep.

If you ride my bumper, I'll ride my brakes.

Truck drivers do it with a full load.

You may have a death wish but I don't – Back Off!

You call it road rage; I call it aggressively moving around morons who don't know how to drive.

Chapter 8: Summary

Hey, that's pretty well it for this book. I hope you've enjoyed it.

I've written a few other joke books for other professions, and here are just a few jokes from my electricians joke book:-

Q: What kind of van does an electrician drive?

A: A *Volts-wagon.*

Q: What do you call a Russian electrician?

A: *Switchitonanov.*

Q: What is the definition of a shock absorber?

A: *A careless electrician.*

About the Author

Chester Croker has written many joke books and has twice been voted Comedy Writer Of The Year by the International Jokers Guild

Chester is known to his friends as Croker the Joker and he has driven many roads over the years and has come across many characters, which has helped provide him with plenty of material for this joke book.

If you see anything wrong, or you have a gag you would like to see included in the next version of this book, please visit the glowwormpress.com website.

If you did enjoy the book, kindly leave a review on Amazon so that other truck drivers can have a good laugh too.

Thanks in advance.

Printed in Great Britain
by Amazon